# Reflections
## *and*
# Ironies
*Packaged in Rhyme*

## Pat D'Amico

*A small note of cheer —*
*Love,*
*Pat*

## Illustrated By
## Pete D'Amico

First Edition

ISBN: 0-9650543-0-6
Library of Congress Catalog Card number: 95-092830

Pilot Publications
P. O. Box 3951
Bellevue, Washington 98009-3951

Printed in The United States of America by
Gorham Printing
Rochester, Washington

# Acknowledgements

Thanks to my son, Pete, for perfectly translating my thoughts into visual images and to my daughter Maria, for editing, arranging, and whipping it all into shape.

# Contents

Chapter One.      .      .      .      .      1

All poems in Chapter One have appeared in *The Wall Street Journal.*

Chapter Two.      .      .      .      .      50

All poems in Chapter Two have appeared in the author's notebook.

The *Wall Street Journal* publishes light verse daily. Look for *Pepper...and Salt* on the editorial page.

# Additional Copies of this Book

To order additional copies of *Reflections and Ironies*, please send your name, address, $8.95 per copy, plus $2.00 for shipping and handling to:

Pilot Publications
P. O. Box 3951
Bellevue, WA 98009-3951


Or phone:
(206) 920-1850

# Chapter
## One

## Water Wisdom

Washington crossed the Delaware,
As historical paintings will note,
But even our country's father,
Shouldn't stand up in a boat.

# Rotisserie News

A political story
Is never quite done
Until it's been tasted,
Basted and spun.

# Safety Valves

In the hallowed halls of Congress,
(The crop's elected cream)
There's an awful lot of posturing
And blowing off of steam.
It's physics, plain and simple,
Since hot air creates velocity:
Imagine the explosion
If they punctured their pomposity.

# Spokespersons

The oil goes to
The wheel that squeaks;
The press goes to
The wheel that leaks.

# Watch Yourself!

We're hoping that you'll
Mind the old Golden Rule
And never behave with impunity,
Because with camcorders
Everything borders
On a photo opportunity.

# Frothy

When a person's self importance
Appears to fairly scream,
The chances are he's building up
a head of self esteem.

# Weather Wig-Out

Climate control
Would be useful, I guess
But by the same token
I'm prompted to stress:
If the wind and the rain
Started jumping through hoops,
Just imagine the deluge of interest groups.

## Emotional Outlets

With telecommunication
And less need for human alliances,
You can always call home if you're lonely
And talk to your appliances.

## Platter Matter

Our 78s and our vinyl LPs
Have been made obsolete by our newer CDs,
Proving once more, that just as we thought,
Music's eternal but recordings are not.

## Shopping Intelligence

I have put some things back
That I clearly desired
Because of three words:
"Some assembly required."

## Jangle Bells

There still are vigorous telephone rings
That command everyone to leap -
In contrast to one of those wimpy things
That warble or chirp or beep.

# Teched Off!

They say this computer's so friendly
I'll be tempted to give it a hug.
Wrong!  It made me so mad
That they ought to be glad
All I did was pull it's plug.


# Literary Diehard

A world of knowledge on a leash
Is what we have with microfiche.
Reading screens is for the birds!
I like paper with my words.


# The Good Old Days

I'll admit that I pause
And then ponder and tarry
When I enter our local
Newfangled library.
Computerized systems
Have me in a fog.
Give me decimals by Dewey
And a card catalog.

## Life in the Fax Lane

Forget about chronology
When buying new technology.
As a rule of thumb: It's obsolete
When the payments are complete.

## Holding Patter

I like mellow music;
I relish the news;
A market report
Or editorial views.
But when I'm on hold
I'm often appalled
To find I've forgotten
The reason I called.

## Voice, You Say?

It was a simple business question -
Now this firm has got me fumin':
They bounced me through their voice mail
And I never found a human.

## Hang-Ups

Telemarketers have a way
Of opening with, "How are you today?"
And so I feel it is my task
To answer, "How nice of you to ask!
My car has a flat; I'm getting the flu;
I can't find my cat and my bills are all due."
Then I get a feeling akin to glee
When the telemarketer hangs up on me.

# Ploy Ground

"All you have to do my friend,
Is come in and claim your prize.
Lady Luck has smiled on you -
Isn't that a nice surprise?
You've won a car, a VCR,
Or a pile of cash as well:
And quite coincidentally -
We have property to sell."

# Volume Control

Commercials keep shouting
Whatever they're touting,
Although it would be more astute
To realize the noise
Causes fingers to poise
Directly over the "mute."

# Camera Shy

You will know an avid photographer
By virtue of this stricture:
He is the one who never appears
In any family picture.

# Crock Pot

A respected scientific group
Says we came from primordial soup.
It follows then - no ifs, ands or buts -
We surely have gone from soup to nuts.


# Straight Arrow

The divorce rate is rising
And it's not surprising,
The excuses are getting lame.
But, hey, we're not stupid,
Let's blame it on Cupid
And his unfortunate aim.


# Too Late to File

When a person approaches the Pearly Gate
And is hoping to get into Heaven,
Let's hope his earthly accounts are straight.
It's too late for a Chapter Eleven.

## A Hard Day's Bite

At the end of the day when we've been away
Stalking the corporate beast
We return to the nest hoping to rest
And share in a hard-earned feast.
We're too tired to cook so we hungrily look
Through the house with primeval anxiety.
We eat what we find and again, we're aligned
With a hunting-and-gathering society.

## Contradiction in Terms

Their product is made to last.
They advertise its endurance.
Why then, are they so fast
To sell us repair insurance?

# Hard Cover Happiness

There are always people coming up
With innovative notions
About the way in which we should
Get in touch with our emotions.
After we have read their books,
We are often twice as tense.
We should have saved our dollars
And used our common sense.


# All Bragged Out

The era, we're told,
Is finally ending
Where yuppies are yapping
About all their spending!


# Piece Corps

The product was made in the U.S.A.,
A concept that's close to our hearts.
It's just that they had to send away
For all its components and parts.

# The Buck Stops Here

Books and tapes of business schemes
That play upon our hopes and dreams,
Seem to mainly fill the cup
Of the ones who thought them up.

# Take a Break

When the market's a bummer
And you couldn't feel glummer,
And your head aches, which makes it worse,
Take a little vacation
Of one minute's duration
To this page and engage in light verse.

# Corporate Castmates

They threw a party to send him off,
With gifts and recognition,
But soon they had to fend him off -
He became the competition!

## Wall Street

When I was just a child
And confronted by my fears,
The things that I thought would get me
Had fangs and pointed ears.
Nothing much has changed -
My periodic scares
Are still from hostile animals,
Only now they're bulls and bears.

# Road's Caller

There's a rich financier
With a phone in his ear,
From his car, a contract he's sealing.
"The deal's in the bag,"
I heard him brag.
He is literally wheeling and dealing.


# Fret of the Vine

Beware of the wine
From an office grapevine,
Though temptation is undeniable:
But as often is true
With that kind of a brew,
The product is unreliable.


# A Ripple of Enthusiasm

As the boss strolls through the office
There are movements that are jerky,
Everyone is sitting up and trying to look perky.
When he has passed on by they all begin to cave -
It's the corporate rendition
Of the sports arena "wave."

# Power Tools

At power breakfasts
And power lunches
Business people
Meet in bunches.
Near the potted palms
We see them lurking.
There's no time for eating -
They're too busy networking.

# Workplace Wisdom

To forgive is divine -
By this I'm inspired.
To err, though it's human,
Can get you fired.

# Committee Coma

The meeting's so dull
That when there's a lull,
It's hard not to notice or mention
That eyelids are lifting
On those who were drifting,
And everyone snaps to attention.

# A Walking Billboard

There used to be some mystery
About each fellow human:
His hobby picks, his politics,
His level of acumen.
Now to find what's on his mind,
It takes no expertise.
We only need to stop and read
His views in T-shirt-ese.

# Self Steam

Those who rejoice
In the human voice
Are certainly not alone.
But sad to say,
They end up that way
When they only rejoice in their own.

# Good Point

This is a fact of life
Upon which I always will harp:
It's easy to cut your own throat
If your tongue is becoming too sharp.

# A Scientific Explanation

In people who always get testy
When faced with stress and strain,
The adrenalin pumps straight to the mouth
Without ever passing the brain.

# Going Concern

Your footprints in the sands of time
Will be a lot more fitting
Than impressions you would make
If you were always sitting.

# Drifters

If you go with the flow
And never quite care,
You could find yourself
Washed up somewhere.

# Gray Matter

Too many options, too many voices
Are inundating me with choices.
Sometimes it seems like right and wrong
Are made up as we go along.

## Motion Operandi

In an elevator between the floors,
Sooner or later each face implores:
I'll stare at my spot -You stare at yours.

## Biting Truth

Some trusting assumptions
Are foolish and witless,
Like the careless consumption
Of olives marked "pitless."
If you must persist
The results can be ruthless:
Cease and desist
Or you may be toothless.

# Under the Sauce

I'm thinking back to the days
Before it was so tony -
We ate a lot of pasta,
But we called it macaroni!

# Discomfort Foods

When baby boomers are under the weather,
They eat the foods that they hope will tether
Them back to the days when life was more mellow
With alphabet soup and strawberry Jell-O.
But pity the next generation of tykes -
Craving tofu and bean sprouts when illness strikes!

# Appetite Depressant

Nouvelle cuisine
Has often been seen
As a work of art on a plate.
It's not very hearty
When served at a party,
And you can't be sure that you ate.

# Expresso Bars

Sitting or standing
Or perched on a stool,
The corporate world
Lines up for its fuel.
Forget about OPEC
And look to the bean -
The runners of commerce
Run on caffeine.

# Book of Life, A.M. Edition

Is your tardiness giving you grief
And you sense unemployment hovers?
In order to turn a new leaf,
You must first turn back the covers.

# Dietary Don'ts

The doctors these days are finding fault
With sugar and coffee and fat.
We would take it all with a grain of salt
But we can't even have that.

# Eye-Opener

I am tired and cranky,
But I will be less so
As soon as I get me
A shot of espresso!

# Then and Now

The value of money has changed -
That's the truth, and here is the brunt of it:
I paid less for the house I've been living in
Than for the car that's parked in the front of it.

# Selective Sizing

A man's home is his castle,
But it often seems lesser
When describing it to
The tax assessor.

# A Change of Scenery

To my mountain retreat (a tiny abode)
A city street has replaced a dirt road;
And parcels of land have been shaved into lots;
Gargantuan houses have slipped into slots.
The neighborhood's upscale, trendy and grooving -
As quick as I can, I will be moving!

# Dogged Dilemma

We all know that man's best friend
Does not make judgments or pretend;
And there've been times, I must confide,
When man and beast sit side by side,
I can't make up my mind for sure
Which one should get off the furniture.

# TV Tuber

Let's see if I have this right:
Couch potatoes are now communing
By staying at home at night
And spending their time cacooning?
There's one thing that I foresee -
Without very many doubts -
The end result will likely be
A proliferation of sprouts.

# Kids Will Be Kids

Could I have a tantrum
If something gets me riled
and blame the consequences
On my inner child?

# Tax for Tots

Hey there, kid in the diaper,
Your piggy bank's overflowing.
It's time now to pay the piper -
Your taxable interest is growing.
So, ante up, little tykes,
Or I would venture a guess
You will find that your little trikes
Have been seized by the IRS.

## No Thanks for the Memory

If I should forget myself
And do something rather dumb,
It will be a certainty
That in the years to come
There will be some person
In whose mind remains an ember -
And it will be his mission
To be sure that I remember.

## Destination Unknown

If our students are poor in geography,
As was shown in a recent quiz,
How can they get where they want to be
When they don't even know where it is?

## Loose Ends

Now I must capitulate
And finish all the jobs I hate.
The race is on and we'll soon see
If I get to them or they get to me.

## Puff Piece

The kids who sneaked their smokes,
When behind the barn they'd traipse,
Are now the very same folks
Who puff on fire escapes.

## Slip of the Lip

Why did I have to volunteer
For this project that I am now christening?
Once again, it's absolutely clear
That I talked when I should have been listening.

# Exit Lines

As a rule of thumb for houseguests,
Try to look at it this way:
The time for leaving is best
While they're still urging you to stay.


# Face Value

My face will contort
And my brain will cavort
In a place that is out of my reach
As soon as I stand
With my notes in my hand
To deliver some kind of a speech.


# Northern Exposure

One of the little curses
Of writing newspaper verses
Is that these very pages
Could line tomorrow's bird cages.
However there is a chance,
In just the right circumstance,
That they may be read once more
On a refrigerator door.

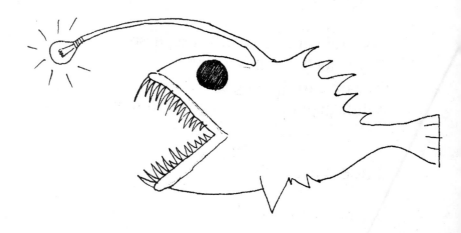

## Two Headed Monster

Easy credit lures us
Into frivolous excesses.
The same voice that assures us
Also repossesses!

# Breaking Loose

The climate is rough
And reoccurring squalls
Are blowing the anchors
Right off of their malls.


# High Rise Prices

Regarding lawyers' offices,
This will not come as news:
Commanding fees are commensurate
With commanding views.


# Legal Gibberish

When lawyers speak in "legalese,"
It's a symphony of expertise -
But the ways in which their words are strung
Sometimes belie our mother tongue.

## Mannequins

The models who slink down the runway
Are always so lean and lanky.
I'm guessing they're probably hungry -
And that's why they look so cranky.

## Glazed Over

The sticky, sweet behavior
That is poured quite frequently
Is often to court favor
Rather syrup-titiously.

## Doll of No Recall

Oh, Barbie and Ken,
I knew you when
You appeared in the social scheme.
Even in those days,
Your yuppie ways
Were every little girl's dream.
More is the pity,
You got broken and gritty,
So somehow or other we parted.
Now your worth is respectable,
Now you're collectible
Leaving me brokenhearted.

## Drift Dodger

I have run the gamut swiftly,
I've dodged those who lay in wait;
I've ignored their warmest smiles,
I have passed up all their bait.
Those who are less fleet of foot
Are always getting blitzed
But I got through the perfume aisle
And didn't once get spritzed.

# Fitness Fits

At the gym you should stay
Out of everyone's way
When man and machine are both straining;
And if you interfere
Or refuse to stand clear,
You will know what they mean by "cross" training.


# Gym-Dandy

When birds of a feather
Work out together,
They all heed the call and the chirp
Of the Headband-Crested
Lycra-Chested
Urban Aerobic Twerp.


# Firming It Up

I have formed a firm philosophy
About exercise devices:
I do not have to use them -
Just owning them suffices.

# Confusion Afoot

O.K. so I'm dated
But it has to be stated:
There used to be fitness gurus
Who were good at all sports
Of various sorts
Without any special shoes.


# Futile Attraction

Since gender issues are complex
And fashions now are unisex,
The young must find it disconcerting
To make mistakes when they are flirting.


# Pair Pressure

We've heard it all now -
The kid has the blues,
Seeing as how
There's no air in his shoes.

# Hold the Putty

With lipsticks, liners, lotions and creams,
There are still beauty plans left to tackle:
But as the years go by, it seems
That before I paint, I should spackle!

# Grunge Proof

From this fashion extreme
I am perfectly safe -
There is no way on earth
I could look like a waif.

# Age Limits

When somebody says, "You're looking good,"
I know these days it's understood:
Considering the years I span,
I'm looking about as good as I can.

# Ambiguous Chic

A business suit, somehow,
Just doesn't hack it
When the skirt ends two inches
Below the jacket.

# Driver's Education

When the kids hit their teens,
I have noticed, in essence,
They are not very keen
On parental presence -
But their permits to drive
Make us once again tight
And I always am welcome -
Front seat, right.


# Lettered and Unfettered

The fast cars that are passing me
Have names that start with X Y Z,
While I remind myself again
That my car's name is L M N.


# Road Gamblers

Some drivers I know can be helplessly lost
And ignore all the help that is beckoning.
They won't ask directions at any cost,
And rely on extremely dead reckoning.

# Idiot's Delight

The driver ahead is meandering,
Laughing and talking and gandering.
He'll snap to attention and give it the gas
The minute he senses I'm trying to pass.

## Bumper Snicker

I'm driving behind you
And I'd like to record
Thät I don't care
Whom you have on board.
I'd be just as careful
If you didn't dangle
Your passenger list
On a double triangle.

## Beyond the Veil

The curtain has closed -
Let us raise a glass
To the lucky devils
Flying first class.

# Plane Pests

The people who can't sit still
And are constantly on their feet -
Invariably will, on an airplane,
Request a window seat.

# Armrest Wrestling

Since it cannot be divided,
How on earth is it decided
At a concert or a play,
Which elbow goes and which can stay?

# Fan's Immunity

Spectator sports, it seems to me,
Are an excellent form of therapy.
Where else can you publicly scream and yell
And not find yourself locked up in a cell.

# Redundant Decor

I like coffee table books
So much, I'm hardly able
To find a spot where I can put
A cup upon the table.

# Censored Sellout

Some of the worst artistic junk
That a prudent public would usually debunk
Will become a hit as quick as a flash
The minute the censors label it trash!

# Picture This

At a sporting event
Or a musical show
Where children perform
And parents go,
You'll find a contingent
along the borders
Vying for space
With all their camcorders.

## Off-the-Wall Opinion

No time should we waste
Accounting for taste
In the paintings some critics acclaim.
Let's agree from the start
That to someone, it's art -
As soon as it's put in a frame.

## Only Children Allowed

Pop psychologists seem to be riled
About getting in touch with one's inner child.
The thing that the experts ought to get real with
Is few of us need more children to deal with.

## Writers, Where Are You?

In violent movies
Nine times out of ten
The sword is mightier
Than the pen.

## Plain Sense

Concerning uplifting adages,
I think it's safe to bet:
If a smile is one's umbrella,
One's certain to get wet.

## Absentee Artist

When I stare off into space
And look like nobody's home,
Don't go away,  I'll be right back!
I'm out composing a poem.

## Slave to Love

I stand in the rain like a nincompoop -
In one hand a leash, in the other a scoop.
I'm happy to be a significant cog
Revolving around the love of a dog.

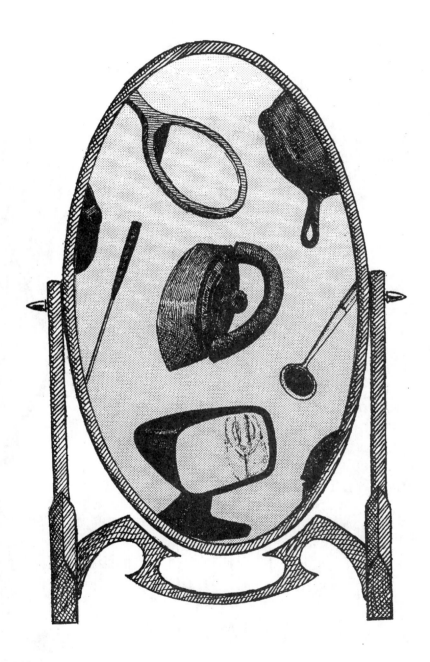

# Oh, Christmas Tree

My mother is sweet,
I learned poise at her feet,
Her disposition is level.
No matter how bad,
She never gets mad,
Her control would confound the devil.
Until what did I see
But a Christmas tree
That wouldn't stand on its own.
It was bangled and baubled
As it wiggled and wobbled -
The star on the top brightly shone.
She was very nice,
She straightened it twice
And then about twenty times more.
Then before I knew it
She hauled off and threw it
Directly out the back door!
As the tree hit the lawn,
The ornaments rolled on -
Even the crash didn't dim it.
I learned that day
In a graphic way
That even a saint has a limit.

# Chapter Two

# A Gym Dandy Idea

Little Ms. Muffet
Got off her tuffet
And hopped on an exercise bike.
Along came a rider
Who worked out beside her
And thought up a plan that I like.
"I propose," said he
(A Grad. of MIT
And a certified innovator)
"That we use all this vim
And connect every gym
To some kind of a generator."
The surplus of power
Produced by the hour
Would crank up a lot of juice,
And the trimming of thighs
Would light the night skies " -
So help me, Mother goose!

# Printed Pique

Many a politician
Has ranted, raved and emoted,
Only to find when he's calmer of mind
That he has already been quoted.

# Open and Shut Face

I wish that God had included
Some special controlling device
To help out those cranky humans
Who find it hard to be nice;
So just as they open their mouths
To deliver some unkind cut
By the magic of automation
Their mouths are swiftly slammed shut!

# Prevailing Breeze

Wherever one walks,
North, south, up or down,
There's a breeze from behind
In a hospital gown.

# Going Out With the Girls

An old lady who never was married
Declared how she wished to be buried:
"To Heaven or Hades, give me pall bearing ladies,
I'm particular how I am carried.
In my lifetime," she said with a pout,
"No man ever cared about
How much I was pining for wining and dining -
It's too late to be taking me out!"

# Half Baked Solution

Andrew McCorkle grabbed his snorkel
And dashed for a tropical beach.
He sat in the sand and thought he'd get tanned
But Andrew turned pink as a peach.
In the sun's rays we watched Andrew braise
And wondered if it would be rude
To approach a stranger and say, "You're in danger,"
Or could it be misconstrued?
So there Andrew lay in a lotion saute'
Intensifying his hue.
His friends didn't mind or else they were blind-
They slapped on a little more goo.
We were caught up in quarrels of ethics and morals
When Andrew called it a day.
He was red as a melon and there is no tellin'
The price that Andrew will pay.

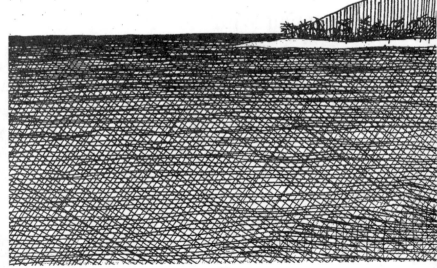

# The New Me

Paved with good intentions,
Is the road to you know where;
So I'll not touch a cookie,
candy, cake or an eclair.
I'll organize my closet,
Wash my car and clean my drawers;
I'll never leave the office
Till I've finished all my chores.
I'll exercise and energize
Till I am strong and sleek.
I am so enthusiastic
That I just may start next week!


# Some Assembly Required

Fit slot A in slot B
Then attach C to D:
The directions are clearly defined.
With just household tools
They've made babbling fools
Of the "mechanically disinclined!"

# The Devil, You Say

He is usually dressed in black.
He has hidden his horns and his tail.
I repel him, but he will be back.
He knows my resistance is frail.
He's confident that he will win,
(He always does sooner or later)
But today I resolve to be thin -
"Be gone, you dessert cart waiter!"

# A Punky-Do

Hair that is purple or pink and blue,
Shaved or all spiked with some styling goo
Leaves an observer with little doubt
That the head is unusual - inside and out.

# Hair Today....

We whine as we say,
"It's a bad hair day,"
While we know in our hearts we will find
Those who fear that their fate
Is a balding pate
Bless a hair day of any kind.

# An Identity Problem

Her eye color changed with contacts;
Her hair color, "ditto" with dye.
Her height was increased by the heels on her shoes -
Her weight, by banana cream pie.
She was trying to find herself
Till she came to the realization
That nothing about her was still the same
As her driver's identification.

# White Water

I would have to be daft to get in a raft
And shoot down a raging river.
The school of hard knocks in the rapids and rocks
Is no place for this lily liver.
They say it is thrilling but sometimes there's spilling
And I would be willing to bet some
That inevitably, I would be the spillee
And end up as flotsam or jetsam!


# Joined at the Hip

Creeps and thugs
Sell illegal drugs
That forever tie them
To the fools that buy them.


# Stupid Human Tricks

How stupid can humans be
When they try marijuana or crack?
How can they help but see
That reality always comes back?

## Memory Lapse

Here I am - temporarily -
Pausing on the stair.
I was going - momentarily -
To do an errand somewhere.
The problem that's perplexing me
And causing me to frown
Is I can't remember - definitely -
If I was going up or down.

# A Lot of Pluck

Although it is yummy,
A candy that's gummy
Has hastily sent us
To visit the dentist
Where we sheepishly stand
With our inlays in hand.

# Seasonal Mix-Up

Where winter is spring
And summer is fall:
The clothing departments
In stores in the mall.

# A Good Deal

I can get it
For a song
If only the bank
Will hum along.

## Hot Spots

A person who's out of sorts
And looking to vent his ire
Can always find a spark
To fan into a fire.

## Legal Advice

Be a sport,
Thwart the tort
And settle the matter
Out of court!

## Clamming Up

No matter how hard
One seems to be trying,
Relationships never
Open by prying.

## All Shook Up

The movers and shakers
Who cause such sensations
Sometimes come apart
With their own vibrations.

# Train of Thought

Holy onomatopoeia!
How I wish that I could see a
Train like those that I once knew
That runs on steam and goes "choo-choo."

# She's Just Amazing

This woman and I were schoolmates;
She's turned out superior, not just better.
My reference for this conclusion
Is her annual Christmas newsletter.
Her business acumen's amazing
And everyone in the know
Says in her chosen career
She will soon be the CEO.
Her home is tidy and dust free.
I have seen it for myself.
When no one was looking I even peeked
On top of the bookcase shelf.
Her children are always polite.
They play "nicely" and are her glory.
Mine have been known to kick and bite
But that is another story.
She polished her PhD thesis
While in labor with child number two.
She would have taken the day off
But she had too much to do.
There is one last thing to mention:
The marathon race that she won.
She planned to be home exactly
When her savory pot roast got done.
She's forging ahead at warp speed
And so this is where I'll leave her -
In the Utopian myth that she's scheduled with -
A perennial overachiever!

# Nostalgia

How I wish I'd kept the comic books
We read when we were kids;
And all the toys we played with
In their boxes with their lids.
To childish things, in middle age,
I find that I aspire -
If I could only have them now,
I'd sell them and retire.

# Sole Survivors

They started out as sole mates,
Now they're single in a box.
Some trouble in the laundry room
Has come between my socks.

# Exuding Good Taste

A bulb of garlic (roasted)
Spread on bread that's toasted
Is sure to fill the air
With more than savoir-faire.

# Sibling Education

Sisters and brothers
With their childish strife
Prepare each other
To face real life
By demonstrating
The traits that vex
The members of
The opposite sex.

# Door Dings

I would love a shiny new car
But my joy would be equally matched
By the consummate worry and unbridled fury
Before and after it's scratched.

# Remote Control

When I'm home alone,
I don't have to dicker -
I'm the undisputed
Queen of the clicker!

# Bittersweet Parting

They all went down in the name of truth
On one melancholy day:
The Easter Bunny, Santa Claus
And the Tooth Fairy faded away.

# Fingerprint Experts

It's tradition with children
When they walk down a hall
To carefully place
Their hands on the wall
So their progress from start
To the other end
Can clearly be traced
By friend after friend.
I seriously doubt
If Lewis and Clark's
Trail to the west
Left more definite marks.

# A Brief Interlude

Out on a boat on a sunny day,
Some dolphins joined us in vigorous play.
They gave us a feeling, too strong to miss,
That God said, "Hang in there!" and gave us a kiss.

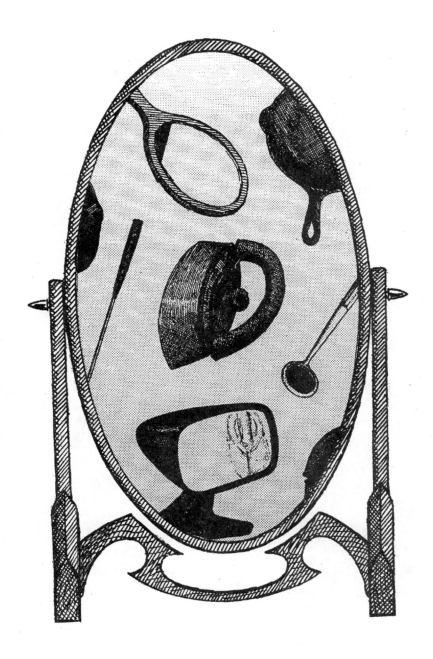

# Additional Copies of this Book

To order additional copies of *Reflections and Ironies*, please forward your name, address and $8.95 per copy plus $2.00 shipping and handling to:

Pilot Publications
P. O. Box 3951
Bellevue, WA 98009-3951

Or phone:
(206) 920-1850